Truth and Rumors
Mummies

by Heather L. Montgomery   illustrations by Eldon Doty

Consultant:
Salima Ikram, PhD
Egypt Archaeologist

CAPSTONE PRESS
a capstone imprint

Edge Books are published by Capstone Press,
151 Good Counsel Drive, P.O. Box 669, Mankato, Minnesota 56002.
www.capstonepress.com

Printed in the United States of America in Stevens Point, Wisconsin.
092009
005619WZS10

Books published by Capstone Press are manufactured with paper
containing at least 10 percent post-consumer waste.

Library of Congress Cataloging-in-Publication Data
Montgomery, Heather L.
    Mummies : truth and rumors / by Heather L. Montgomery ; illustrated by Eldon Doty.
    p. cm. — (Edge books. Truth and rumors)
    Includes bibliographical references and index.
    Summary: "Labels common stories about mummies as fact or fiction and teaches readers how to
tell the difference between truth and rumors" — Provided by publisher.
    ISBN 978-1-4296-3950-7 (library binding)
    1. Mummies — Juvenile literature. I. Doty, Eldon, ill. II. Title. III. Series.
GN293.M66 2010
393'.3 — dc22   2009028653

Editorial Credits

Abby Czeskleba, editor; Tracy Davies; designer; Wanda Winch, media researcher;
    Nathan Gassman, art director; Laura Manthe, production specialist; Eldon Doty, illustrator

Photo Credits

Alamy: Danita Delimont/Kenneth Garrett 8 (bottom); AnimationNation.com: Charles Zembillas
25 (bottom); The Bridgeman Art Library: ©Look and Learn/Private Collection/Sinking of the
Titanic 18 (top); Corbis: Reuters/Peter Andrews 23 (bottom), Reuters/Pilar Olivares 20 (top); The
Denver Public Library Western History/Genealogy Dept. 14 (top); Getty Images Inc.: AFP/Sam Yeh
19 (bottom); Griffith Institute, University of Oxford 10 (bottom); iStockphoto: Bill Noll cover
(blue texture); Library of Congress 24 (top); Mary Evans Picture Library 8 (top); Newscom: 12
(bottom), 20 (bottom), AFP/Claudio Santana 26, AbacaPress.com/Itar-Tass/Andrei Tkachev 17
(bottom), AFP/Khaled-Dessouki Mena 6 (bottom), NGS/Grave Secrets of Dinosaurs/MCT 16;
Capstone: Picture Window Books/Steve Watson 17 (top); Shutterstock: Adam Radosavljevic back
cover (frame), cover (square frames), Albachiara (quill pen/inkwell, throughout), Ali Mazraie Shadi
(halftone throughout), Bruno ismael da silva alves front, back cover (desert floor), Dragana
Jokmanovic front, back cover (background), GTibbetts 13 (top), hektor2 cover (round frame), Jarno
Gonzalez Zarraonandia cover (mummy center), Timur Kulgarin cover (papyrus left), VikaSuh (gavel,
throughout); Wikimedia: 12 (top), Captmondo cover (mummy right), 29 (top)

Table of Contents

Mummies . . . What's Real?

Footsteps follow you down a dark hallway. You glance back — it's a mummy! With its arms in front of its body, it stares at you with wide-open eyes. As the mummy comes closer, it reaches out to grab you. You quickly bolt down the hallway with the mummy close behind.

Luckily, that kind of mummy story is made up. But mummies and their stories can be real. Sometimes, it's not easy to tell if a story is true. In fact, most rumors are based on some facts.

How can you tell if the stories you hear are real? You have to be a detective and collect **evidence** to decide which parts to believe. If you pay attention to a story's details, you may be able to tell what's real. This book gives you plenty of stories to test your skills.

evidence – information, items, and facts that help prove something is true or false

Were mummies used as medicine?

What's the story?

Beginning in the 1200s, people ground up mummies into powder. Sometimes they ate the powder as medicine. This practice lasted for 500 years.

Oliver's organic MUMMY POWder

THE EVIDENCE

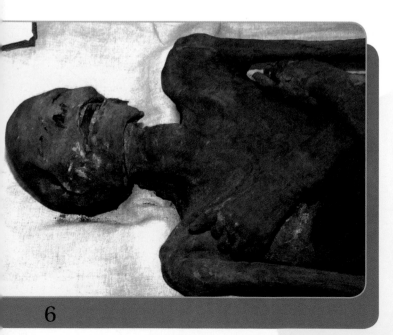

Egyptian mummies looked like they were coated in asphalt. They were called mumia, which means "natural asphalt." Some people thought old medical books suggested using mumia as medicine. But the books really said to use asphalt.

Europeans wanted medicine to relieve their pain. Doctors gave patients powder from ground-up mummies. The mummy powder was used to treat headaches, wounds, and stomachaches. Records show that mummies were commonly shipped from Egypt to Europe during this time.

FACT: Drug stores quickly ran out of fingers, feet, and other mummy parts to make mummy powder. People then started mummifying any dead body they could find in Egypt.

The VERDICT

Yes. A misunderstanding led to the practice of making medicine from mummies. People really did eat powder made from dead, rotting bodies. In those days, no one knew about germs.

MUNCH MUNCH

MUMMY POWDER

Delicious! Slightly fruity with a hint of mustard and ash

7

Was King Tut murdered?

What's the story?

Eighteen-year-old King Tutankhamen of Egypt was killed by someone who wanted his throne. The killer might have been the king's advisor, a man named Ay. Because Tut was 8 years old when he became king, Ay made many decisions for the king.

THE EVIDENCE

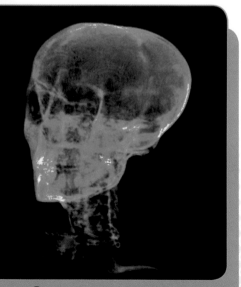

In 1968, x-rays of Tut's body showed a dark spot on his skull. One expert claimed the hole was caused by a blow to the head. The x-rays led people to believe King Tut was murdered.

Years later, a computer scan showed the spot was a hole. Bits of bone lay inside his skull. Was the hole evidence of murder? Or maybe the **embalmers** made the hole while preparing the body more than 3,000 years ago.

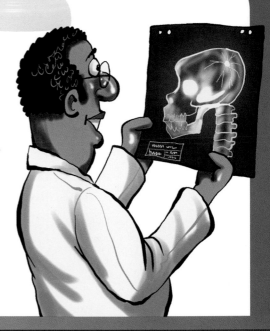

No. The early x-rays showed damage to Tut's head. Researchers looking at the x-rays thought that the wound happened while Tut was alive. But years later, researchers learned the hole was made after King Tut's death. The embalmers may have dropped the body. The bits of bone most likely fell into the skull.

embalmer – a person who preserves a dead body so it does not decay

Ancient Egyptian Mummification

To mummify a body, Egyptian embalmers first removed the brain. They used a sharp rod to break the brain into tiny pieces. Embalmers used another tool to turn the pieces into liquid. Finally, they used a hooked object to pull the brain out through a nostril. Embalmers also removed the intestines, stomach, liver, and lungs. The heart was the only organ left in the body.

Removing body parts was only the beginning. The embalmers also washed the body to keep it from smelling and to kill germs. After the bath, the body was dried with a salt mixture called natron. Bags of natron were also placed inside the body.

After the 40-day drying process, the embalmers rubbed oil on the body to help the arms and legs move more easily. Without the oil, body parts would snap off because they were so dry. Finally, the body was sealed with linen and resin.

9

Is King Tut's tomb cursed?

What's the story?

People say a curse is carved above King Tut's tomb. It reads: "Death shall come on swift wings to him that touches the tomb of the Pharaoh." The curse is believed to be responsible for the deaths of those who've entered the tomb.

THE EVIDENCE

In the early 1920s, people watched as Lord Carnarvon and **archaeologist** Howard Carter opened King Tut's tomb. Trouble started the moment Carter opened the tomb. Back at his home, a snake swallowed his pet canary.

Then the curse killed Lord Carnarvon, the man who paid for Carter's trip to Egypt. When Carnarvon died, the lights across the city of Cairo went out. Half of the people who were at the tomb's opening also died years later.

10

No. You'd know this story is full of fibs if you had watched Carter open the tomb. For starters, there is no warning written on King Tut's tomb. Historians don't know if a snake really ate Carter's canary. Lord Carnarvon died, but it was months after the tomb was opened. Plus, the electricity in Cairo often went out during the 1920s.

Most of the people who watched Carter open the tomb lived at least 15 more years. Many people lived into their 60s.

archaeologist – a scientist who studies how people lived in the past

The Legend of the Curse — EXPOSED!

It was a big deal when Howard Carter entered King Tut's tomb. The gold and gems Carter found drew reporters from around the world. But Carter would only talk to reporters writing for London's paper *The Times*.

The special interview with *The Times* upset other reporters. *The New York Times* published a letter that predicted everyone involved in the tomb's opening would die. The letter was written by Marie Corelli, a fiction writer. Corelli said the prediction came from an old Arabic book. Most people probably would have ignored Corelli's letter, but Lord Carnarvon died shortly after it was published. If it weren't for his untimely death, people may have never believed a curse existed.

Did trains burn mummies for fuel?

What's the story?

The Egyptian railroads burned mummies as fuel for steam engines. But where would people get such a strange idea? Author Mark Twain discussed it in his 1869 book *The Innocents Abroad*.

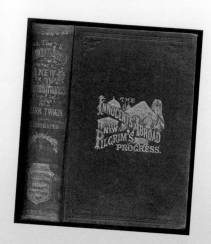

THE EVIDENCE

Egyptian mummies are tightly wrapped in easily burnable materials like dried cloth and resin. Twain wrote about traveling in Egypt. In the book, he explained, ". . . the fuel they use for the locomotive is composed of mummies three thousand years old, purchased by the ton or by the graveyard . . ." Describing this story, Twain also wrote, "I only tell it as I got it. I am willing to believe it. I can believe anything."

No. Steam engines used coal as fuel, not mummies. Mark Twain was a famous fiction writer. In other words, his stories weren't real.

FACT: Grave robbers and tourists used mummy arms as torches.

MUMMY FUEL

CAIRO EXPRESS

Did people catch cholera from mummy linen?

What's the story?

Today, we use fibers from trees to make paper. In the 1850s, factory workers used fibers from cloth to make paper. When cloth supplies started running low, workers began using the linen from mummies. Grocers wrapped food with the mummy paper and people got **cholera**.

NOT SO FAST . . .

Bags of rags were cheap. Buying mummies for their linen would've been expensive. It wouldn't have made sense to spend thousands of dollars when cheap rags were available.

The VERDICT

No. No one has ever found mummy paper used by grocers. Most of the claims about it were made by a person who was known for lying. Besides, cholera is usually spread through human and animal waste. The bacteria that cause the sickness need to stay wet. In a dry mummy, the bacteria would have died. Some paper could have been made from mummy linen, but no one ever got cholera from the paper.

cholera – a disease that causes severe sickness and diarrhea

Is a dinosaur the oldest mummy?

What's the story?

In 1999, 16-year-old Tyler Lyson found the oldest-known mummy in North Dakota. The mummy, named Dakota, was a dinosaur that lived more than 65 million years ago.

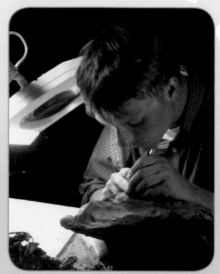

THE EVIDENCE

If the conditions are just right, a body can naturally become a mummy. About 40,000 years ago, a baby mammoth fell into the water and was quickly frozen. Several bodies have been found in bogs. The acid in bogs killed germs and preserved the bodies for thousands of years. Even today, bodies buried in the desert dry out and turn into mummies.

In the case of Dakota, nature turned the dinosaur into a mummy and later into a **fossil**.

> **fossil** – the remains or traces of plants and animals that are preserved as rock

Yes. A duck-billed hadrosaur named Dakota is the oldest known mummy. When the dinosaur died near a river, wet sand covered its body. The sand and water mixture preserved the dinosaur's body. Dakota's skin, muscles, and some organs were still around more than 65 million years after the dinosaur had died.

FACT: Scientists believe Dakota may have weighed more than 3 tons (2.7 metric tons).

Scientists study a frozen baby mammoth that was found in Siberia in 2007.

Did a mummy sink *Titanic*?

What's the story?

In the 1890s, four British men found the mummy of Princess Amen-Ra. Three of the four men died strange, mysterious deaths. The mummy eventually went to the British Museum. Museum workers realized the mummy was cursed and quickly tried to get rid of it. The mummy was sent to an American museum on *Titanic*. Some people believe Princess Amen-Ra sent the ship to its watery grave.

CONSIDER THIS . . .

Some people say the mummy was seeking revenge for being moved from her final resting place. Every person who came in contact with the unlucky mummy became ill or died suddenly.

I'll get you!

The man who delivered Amen-Ra to the British Museum died within a week. Another man took a photo of the mummy, looked at the picture, and then killed himself. With a history of cursing people, it would make sense that the mummy would also doom *Titanic*, right?

The VERDICT

No. There was no mummy on *Titanic*. The British Museum never had the mummy of Princess Amen-Ra. But the museum does have a coffin lid of an unknown priestess.

Did Incan mummies curse people?

What's the story?

In 1999, archaeologists dug up bundles of 500-year-old Incan mummies. For two years, the scientists dug in Tupac Amaru, a town near Lima, Peru. When the archaeologists got sick, people said it was a curse. The mummies' curse also made the townspeople sick.

BUT CONSIDER THIS . . .

Long before the scientists started digging, Tupac Amaru was a peaceful town. In the late 1980s, the town's population grew. But Tupac Amaru had no sewage system for people's waste. As a result, water seeped into the once-dry ground.

The archaeologists began digging because the water was causing the mummies to rot. Didn't the scientists know that digging up an Incan cemetery wasn't a good idea? The scientists developed skin problems, stomachaches, and bad coughs. One boy even died during the project.

FACT: The graveyard near Lima is one of the largest Incan cemeteries in Peru.

The VERDICT

No. Because Tupac Amaru didn't have a sewage system, the waste soaked into the dirt. It was germs, not a mummy's curse, that made the archaeologists sick.

One boy did die during the project. Scientists think he had tuberculosis and was sick before the digging began. But that didn't stop some people from claiming it was a curse.

Is Vladimir Lenin's mummy a fake?

What's the story?

Vladimir Lenin was a Russian hero. When he died in 1924, the Soviets put his mummy on display. Then his skin began to mold. Not wanting to admit that his body was decaying, officials replaced it with a wax figure.

I'm sorry, this is closed!

Perhaps you would like to see the other exhibits.

THE EVIDENCE

Russian officials refused to say how they preserved Lenin's body. That made everyone suspicious. During the construction of a new exhibit building, Lenin's body disappeared. When it showed up again, his wrinkles had vanished. His left hand, which had been clenched tightly, was now open. His skin also looked waxy. People said it could not have been the real Lenin.

The government called in a German scientist to check the body. He said it was the real thing, but not everybody believed him.

No. Lenin's mummy is real. Scientists and staff work to keep Lenin's body looking good. He gets chemical baths that last for two weeks. His face looks waxy because they injected wax to remove the wrinkles.

Is Walt Disney's mummy hidden in Disneyland?

What's the story?

That creepy character in the Haunted House at Disneyland could be Walt Disney himself. OK, maybe that's not completely true. But some people believe Disney's body is buried somewhere in Disneyland.

CONSIDER THIS . . .

Other people say Disney wanted his body to be frozen by **cryonics**. Why? Because Disney hoped to one day come back to life. Perhaps he wanted to live as long as his famous characters.

cryonics – the deep-freezing of a human body shortly after a person dies

The VERDICT

No. Walt Disney was **cremated**. His ashes are in a family plot in Hollywood Hills, California. Cryonics had not even been used on a person until after Disney died in 1966. Disney's daughter said her father had never even heard of it.

How did the rumors start? No one knows for sure, but some people say Disney employees dreamed it up. Maybe workers from another amusement park wanted to scare people away from Disneyland. Or perhaps writers added this story to improve sales of their books about Disney. No one really knows.

cremate – to burn a dead body to ashes

FACT: Famous Red Sox baseball player Ted Williams is a modern mummy. His body was frozen through cryonics.

INSERT BODY HERE

Walt Disney's family burial plot

Did upset mothers make the first mummies?

What's the story?

In South America, heartbroken mothers peeled the skin off their dead babies. The babies became the first man-made mummies.

THE EVIDENCE

Mummy experts thought Egyptians were the first to make mummies 5,000 years ago. But in the 1980s, child mummies were found in the desert of Chile. Scientists believe those mummies were made 7,000 years ago.

Why were the babies mummified in the first place? Maybe a mother could not stand to give up her child, even if he was dead. She pulled the baby's skin off and removed his organs. Then she filled the space with plants, fur, and clay. She put the skin back on, added a mask and wig, and painted the body black. The body became preserved in the dry climate.

Maybe. We can't prove that upset mothers were the first mummy-makers. But someone in Chile made the first mummies 2,000 years before the Egyptians did.

Making Mummies

Mummies are made in different ways around the world. In Australia, people dried dead bodies with fire. In the United States, a train robber's body was filled with arsenic. Then it was put on display at a carnival.

Today, dead bodies are preserved to study. Museums have human bodies preserved with plastic. Some consider the display educational, some call it art, and some say it's disgusting.

ELMER... THE ARSENIC MUMMY

FACT OR FICTION?:
How to Tell the Difference

If you can't always believe everything you read or hear, how do you know what to believe? See if you can tell which of these stories is true:

1.) The perfume Sherit was made to smell like a mummy.

2.) Egyptian embalmers sewed mummies' eyes shut.

3.) A boy broke into a mummy coffin at a museum. The mummy turned the boy into a mummy by kissing him.

Answers:
1. True. A scientist created the perfume to match the smells of oils used to preserve a 2,000-year-old mummy. The mummy was a 5-year-old Egyptian girl named Sherit.
2. False. Egyptians believed that mummies could see in the afterlife, so they would not have sewn the mummies' eyes shut.
3. False. A mummy can't kiss anyone because it's dead. And we all know mummies can't come back to life.

To sort out the truth from the rumors, research the stories you hear. Contact experts at museums, history centers, and universities to ask questions. It is also good to use books and well-known newspapers. Ask a librarian if you're not sure if a source is trustworthy. Do your research, and you'll have no problem learning the truth.

Glossary

archaeologist (ar-kee-AH-luh-jist) — a scientist who studies how people lived in the past

asphalt (AS-fawlt) — a black tar that is mixed with sand and gravel to make paved roads

cholera (KAH-luhr-uh) — a disease that causes sickness and diarrhea

cremate (KREE-mate) — to burn a dead body to ashes

cryonics (krahy-ON-iks) — the deep-freezing of a person's body shortly after he or she dies

embalmer (im-BALM-uhr) — a person who preserves a dead body so it does not decay

evidence (EV-uh-duhnss) — information, items, and facts that help prove something is true or false

fossil (FAH-suhl) — the remains or traces of plants and animals that are preserved as rock

linen (LIN-uhn) — a cloth made from the flax plant; linen was used to wrap ancient Egyptian mummies.

resin (REZ-in) — a sticky substance that comes from the sap of some trees

Read More

Biskup, Agnieszka. *Uncovering Mummies: An Isabel Soto Archaeology Adventure.* Graphic Expeditions. Mankato, Minn.: Capstone Press, 2010.

Grace, N. B. *Mummies Unwrapped!: The Science of Mummy-Making.* 24/7 Science Behind the Scenes. New York: Franklin Watts, 2008.

Krensky, Stephen. *The Mummy.* Monster Chronicles. Minneapolis: Lerner, 2007.

Internet Sites

FactHound offers a safe, fun way to find Internet sites related to this book. All of the sites on FactHound have been researched by our staff.

Here's all you do:

Visit *www.facthound.com*

FactHound will fetch the best sites for you!

Index